E-Careers

Careers in
Social Media

Stuart A. Kallen

ReferencePoint
Press®

San Diego, CA

About the Author

Stuart A. Kallen is the author of more than 350 nonfiction books for children and young adults. He has written on topics ranging from the theory of relativity to the art of electronic dance music. In 2018 Kallen won a Green Earth Award from the Nature Generation environmental organization for his book *Trashing the Planet: Examining the Global Garbage Glut*. In his spare time he is a singer, songwriter, and guitarist in San Diego.

© 2020 ReferencePoint Press, Inc.
Printed in the United States

For more information, contact:
ReferencePoint Press, Inc.
PO Box 27779
San Diego, CA 92198
www.ReferencePointPress.com

Picture Credits:

Cover: Robert Kneschke/Shutterstock.com

 6: Maury Aaseng
13: wavebreakmedia/Shutterstock.com
30: anandaBGD/iStockphoto.com
37: fizes/Shutterstock.com

LIBRARY OF CONGRESS CATALOGING-IN-PUBLICATION DATA

Name: Kallen, Stuart A., 1955– author.
Title: Careers in Social Media/by Stuart A. Kallen.
Description: San Diego, CA: ReferencePoint Press, Inc., 2020. | Series:
   E-Careers series | Includes bibliographical references and index.
Identifiers: LCCN 2019016231 (print) | LCCN 2019017776 (ebook) | ISBN
   9781682826188 (eBook) | ISBN 9781682826171 (hardback)
Subjects: LCSH: Web site development—Vocational guidance—Juvenile
   literature. | Social media—Management—Vocational guidance—Juvenile
   literature. | Online social networks—Vocational guidance—Juvenile literature.
Classification: LCC TK5105.888 (ebook) | LCC TK5105.888 .K36 2020 (print) |
   DDC 006.7023—dc23
LC record available at https://lccn.loc.gov/2019016231

Contents

Wielding Hashtags and Vlogs

A lot of people spend a lot of time on social media. If they are at work, they might even get into trouble for being glued to their screens while they should be working; however, some jobs require employees to post, like, share, scroll, and tweet their days away. These people are social media professionals. They get paid to provide content, create graphics, manage social media postings, analyze statistics, engineer software and computer systems, and promote products for platforms like Facebook, Twitter, Tumblr, Snapchat, LinkedIn, and Instagram.

Some social media mavens are beloved by millions. YouTube entertainers, or YouTubers, have become some of the biggest celebrities on the Internet. In 2019, YouTube personalities like Jenna Marbles, Markiplier, and Michelle Phan each had over 20 million subscribers. The most successful YouTubers attract billions of hits and earn millions of dollars posting clips about fashion, gaming, and various aspects of their daily lives.

Of course, most YouTubers will not reach this level of success—less than four out of a hundred who try for YouTube fame ever make money. But many earn good money wielding hashtags and @ symbols on social media. These professionals speak a language all their own, working to generate alerts when a topic is gaining traction, checking analytics to understand posting performance, and hiring influencers to promote their brands.

Others who work in social media never tag or tweet in a professional capacity. They provide the software and hardware that social media depends on. These social media pros earn six-figure salaries working as computer network architects, mobile app creators, software engineers, and artificial intelligence engineers.

Working in social media can be very profitable, and new career opportunities are being created every day for those who want to work in this field. As Internet marketing specialist Michael Page writes on his homepage: "Engagement with customers, media and staff through social media is a top priority for most companies. Organizations want to know how to use social media platforms like Facebook, Twitter, LinkedIn and blogging to build their brand and gain market share. This increased focus often means hiring new, specialized talent to lead innovation in this space."

If you are a creative thinker with tech skills—and a good communicator with a penchant for posting—a career in social media might be perfect for you. First you'll need to become familiar with social media platforms—and not just through posting and liking. Since Facebook is the world's most popular site, it is a good place to take a deep dive into the inner workings of social media. Click through all the menus, and read through the privacy and security settings. Learn to create a page for a business, brand, or community group. Study ways to advertise on Facebook and create ads. Explore fund-raisers or start your own charity for a local project.

Social media is all about communication, and blogging is a great way to express yourself. Creating a steady stream of blog posts, tweets, and status updates will help you establish an online presence, gain followers, and build a portfolio that shows off your skills. This will be helpful when seeking employment in the social media industry.

Of course, social media is more than the written word. It is a visual medium that thrives on pictures, videos, and flashy graphics. Therefore, creating eye-catching photos, clever memes, and other imaginative original content can increase your number of followers, shares, likes, and loves. And there is no barrier to entry when

Pay for Jobs in Social Media

Source: Falcon.Io, "Ten Social Media Job Titles," Maxwell Gollin, 2019. www.falcon.io.

it comes to creating your own YouTube channel—you don't need to audition or impress an agent or film director. Even if you don't become the next Jake Paul, Zoella, or other YouTube superstar, you will learn how to shoot and edit vlogs (video blogs) and come to understand ad rates, sponsorships, and other business aspects of the social media industry.

Social media provides plenty of other opportunities for self-education. Many who are already working in social media have created do-it-yourself videos and websites that can point you in the right direction. You can engage with others on LinkedIn and other professional social media platforms, or comment on articles and vlogs by others to establish an online relationship with those who already hold the key to success.

A Job That's Easy to Love

Like social media itself, your possibilities are almost limitless when it comes to opportunities. As social media marketer Lucy Rendler-Kaplan explains on the Social Media Today website: "I love that I am able to be creative daily and be a storyteller. I get really involved with the communities I build for the brand clients I work with and LOVE engaging with fans and truly getting to know them. I love that at any time, you can jump into conversations and interact with people in real time and exchange ideas and thoughts." If you leverage your passion, enthusiasm, and creativity to build your own brand and grow a network, you can blaze a path forward to a job that is easy to love.

Graphic Designer

What Does a Graphic Designer Do?

In 2018 the average American consumer spent five hours a day on a mobile device, according to the analytics firm Flurry. Sixty-eight percent of Facebook users accessed the site using a smartphone or tablet, and nearly 100 percent of those who visited Twitter, Instagram, and Snapchat did so using mobile devices. These figures are good news for graphic designers who specialize in social media marketing (SMM). The multibillion dollar SMM industry depends on eye-popping memes, infographics, banner ads, pop-up ads, and logos for mobile devices.

Graphic designers are also called graphic artists. They combine communication skills with artistic talent to create ads and other visual content that grabs the attention of users who are busily scrolling through their news feeds. Graphic designers use photos, drawings, videos, animations, colors, music, and specific type fonts to produce designs that help companies increase

At a Glance

Graphic Designer

Minimum Educational Requirements
Bachelor's degree in fine arts or graphic design

Personal Qualities
Creative, analytical, good communicator, computer skills, able to understand social media marketing

Certification
Adobe Certified Expert recommended

Working Conditions
In studios at drafting tables and computers; long hours when deadlines loom

Pay
$49,530 median annual salary in 2017*

Number of Jobs
266,300 in 2017*

Future Job Outlook
4–20 percent growth through 2026

* includes all graphic designers working in advertising, public relations, and related computer services

8

consumer awareness of their products and grow their customer base. Those who specialize in SMM understand that ads seen on smartphones and tablets need to feature prominent, easy-to-read fonts, bright colors, and eye-catching photos and animation. Their creative skills include having a keen eye for art and color, an understanding of type fonts, and knowledge of the way logos, photos, and other graphic elements come together in distinctive product designs.

While graphic designers mainly work on computers, most are skilled illustrators who also work with pens, colored pencils, crayons, and paints. When brainstorming with clients, they sketch out rough prototypes of design concepts. After ideas are finalized, graphic designers create ads using industry standard graphic design applications such as Adobe Photoshop, Dreamweaver, Illustrator, and InDesign. However, as graphic designer Jonathan Leahy Maharaj notes on the Silicon Republic website: "Don't think that technology is the answer to all of your problems. It's a tool, but it needs a creative brain to utilize it, otherwise it's useless."

How Do You Become a Graphic Designer?

Education

Most graphic designers develop a love for photography, drawing, painting, and even type fonts when they are in middle or high school. Those thinking of pursuing a career in graphic design can take a number of high school courses, including art, commercial art, computer applications, desktop publishing, web design, and graphic design. These classes help improve students' computer skills and creative thinking as they complete assignments that might include producing posters, party invitations, page layouts, T-shirt designs, memes, paintings, sculptures, and photographic essays.

clients face to face, and learned how to build product brands while meeting deadlines. "In school, you get to design things the way you are feeling in the moment," says Ingram, "whereas at an internship, you may have to design how a 50–60 year-old man with a fishing pole on a boat would feel on Father's Day right after a cold beer. Through this internship, I learned that the best Graphic Designers wear many hats (and wear them well), even though these hats may not always be their own."

Career websites like LinkedIn and Glassdoor have numerous listings for summer internship positions in nearly every region of the country. In some cases interns are hired as full-time employees upon graduation.

Skills and Personality

Graphic designers are creative people who have an intuitive sense of art, color, type fonts, logos, photos, and other graphic elements. They use analytical skills to appraise their work from a customer's viewpoint and have a solid sense of the ways their designs will be received on social media.

Social media is all about storytelling, so graphic designers need to have great communication skills that allow them to instantly convey the messages their clients wish to express. They also work very closely with ad copywriters, photographers, production personnel, and other design teammates, which requires them to speak and write clearly and concisely. Since graphic designers often work under tight deadlines, they also need good time-management skills so they can complete work on multiple projects at different phases of development, all while managing their own stress levels.

Graphic design for social media also requires a degree of humility. You might create a design that ends up being shared by thousands of people, none of whom have any idea that you were personally responsible for the work; however, if your employer receives praise and credit, you know you did your job well.

A graphic designer switches between her tablet and desktop computer as she fleshes out an idea for a client. Graphic designers create eye-popping memes, infographics, banner ads, pop-up ads, and logos for mobile devices.

On the Job

Employers

Graphic designers who specialize in social media marketing are employed by advertising agencies, public relations firms, and specialized design companies. About 20 percent of graphic designers are freelancers, or artists who work for themselves or contract themselves out. Successful freelance graphic designers in this highly competitive field are part designer and part salesperson. They need to keep their current clients satisfied while always seeking out new connections.

Working Conditions

Graphic designers work in studios at drafting tables and computer stations. They may work during regular business hours, and they may occasionally work long nights and/or weekends if they need to meet a looming deadline. Graphic designers often work under the leadership of an art director and might be a part of a design team that consists of photographers, production artists, marketing directors, and executives. When a project is completed, a graphic designer will often present his or her work to the client and listen to the client's feedback. Several rounds may be needed in order to incorporate changes requested by the client before the design is finalized.

Earnings

According to the US Bureau of Labor Statistics (BLS), the median annual income for graphic designers who worked in advertising, public relations, and related computer services in 2017 was $49,530. The median income number is the level at which half of those in this occupation earned more and half earned less. In this occupation it means that those in the bottom 10 percent made less than $28,560, while those in the top 10 percent made more than $83,140. The BLS does not publish figures for self-employed social media graphic designers, but the employment website PayScale reports that digital designers who worked across a variety of media earned an average of $52,375 in 2018.

Opportunities for Advancement

Design firms offer many opportunities for advancement, and some graphic designers may be promoted to art directors. Art directors earned an average of $92,250 in 2017, but because this is a senior-level position, the job is very demanding. Art directors work with many different people, including marketing directors, graphic artists, photographers, and executives. Depending on the company, they develop overall designs for products, packaging, print media, and web-based materials. Art directors must be extremely organized, as it is their job to coordinate production artists, illustrators, and others to complete a project on time and to a client's satisfaction.

What Is the Future Outlook for Graphic Designers?

The BLS reports that in 2017 more than 266,300 people were working in graphic design. The field for all graphic designers was expected to grow slowly—by an average of 4 percent a year through 2026. This number, however, also reflects the shrinking number of graphic design jobs in traditional print media and so is not an accurate measure of opportunities to work in social media. The BLS notes that employment for those who work in what it calls "computer systems graphic design" is expected to grow very rapidly, at a rate of 20 percent by 2026. This high figure is backed by a 2018 survey by the online media company Social Media Examiner, which found that more than 60 percent of more than fifty-seven hundred respondents said they planned to increase their Facebook marketing activity during the following year. Similar figures can be found for Instagram and other social media platforms, which should bode well for those who want to pursue a career in social media graphic design.

Find Out More

AIGA, the Professional Association for Design
233 Broadway, 17th floor
New York, NY 10279
www.aiga.org

AIGA (pronounced "A-I-G-A") was founded in 1914 as the American Institute of Graphic Arts and is the oldest and largest professional graphic design organization. It works to advance design as a professional craft and advocates for a greater understanding of the value of design and designers in government, business, and media.

Color Marketing Group (CMG)

1908 Mount Vernon Ave.
Alexandria, VA 22301
https://colormarketing.org

CMG is made up of color design professionals who work with color as it applies to the marketing of goods and services. Its members interpret, create, forecast, and select colors in order to enhance the function, salability, and quality of manufactured goods.

National Association of Schools of Arts and Design (NASAD)

11250 Roger Bacon Dr., Suite 21
Reston, VA 20190
https://nasad.arts-accredit.org

NASAD has established national standards for undergraduate and graduate degrees in art and design. Students wishing to pursue an art degree from high-quality institutions can select from more than 360 accredited art schools, colleges, conservatories, and universities listed on the website.

UCDA (University & College Designers Association)

199 Enon Springs Rd. West, Suite 400
Smyrna, TN 37167
https://ucda.com

UCDA promotes excellence in visual communications for educational institutions. As a professional trade association, it offers professional development opportunities through conferences, summits, and workshops; a quarterly trade publication/magazine; monthly job postings service; and email messaging lists for both working graphic design professionals as well as design educators.

Social Media Manager

What Does a Social Media Manager Do?

If you follow a celebrity on social media, you probably get numerous updates that include behind-the-scenes photos, their comments and thoughts, links to events or brands they like, and teasers about their new projects. Such detailed and frequent posts often make superstars seem like down-to-earth folks who have lots of free time in which to provide constant information to their millions of fans and followers. Some stars, such as Taylor Swift, are known for creating their own social media posts. But most rely on social media managers, also called engagement coordinators, to create accounts on various sites and keep them current.

While some social media managers work for big stars, most have jobs that are less glamorous. Their

At a Glance

Social Media Manager

Minimum Educational Requirements
Bachelor's degree in communication, journalism, or marketing

Personal Qualities
Computer skills, strong knowledge of social media, good communicator, creative, analytical

Certification
Twitter, Facebook, LinkedIn, or other social media certification

Working Conditions
Long hours, days, nights, and weekends following trends and keeping posts current

Pay
$59,300 median annual salary in 2017*

Number of Jobs
259,600 in 2017*

Future Job Outlook
9 percent growth through 2026*

* includes all public relations specialists, including those who work as social media managers

work involves creating multiple social media accounts for companies that market products on Twitter, Instagram, Facebook, Pinterest, Tumblr, Snapchat, and other platforms. Social media managers post photos, drawings, videos, memes, images, and other content. They are responsible for acting as the voice and personality of their clients and accurately representing their clients' viewpoints. They use their communication skills to write engaging blogs and text messages meant to spark interest in topics relating to the brands they promote. Social media managers are also customer relations specialists who correspond with people who have questions about a product or who comment on the posts.

Some social media managers create their own content, while those who work for larger advertising agencies or major corporations work closely with graphic design teams, photographers, and ad copywriters to do so. On the Econsultancy website, social media manager Pippa Bugg describes how she spends her days working at Oasis Fashions: "[I spend a lot of time] Whatsapp-ing back-and-forth with the social media assistant. . . . There's also a lot of meetings, but not the boring kind." A main reason she likes her job is because "everyone gets to input their ideas and create something from scratch."

Bugg says her friends think her job is easy, but managing numerous social media accounts can be quite challenging. Most social media managers juggle around five to twenty clients. That means they need to be constantly online and thinking up fresh and engaging posts. This is especially important given the fact that most posts have a very short life span, or time in which they are viewed by the largest number of social media users. The average tweet is considered relevant for about fifteen minutes, while a Facebook post has a life of around six hours. Instagram posts are seen by the most people within the first twenty-four hours, while YouTube, Pinterest, and blogs have the longest life span. Little wonder that social media managers work hard to make their posts go viral, which can extend their relevancy for days or even weeks as people share or retweet the content. Social media manager Lucy Rendler-Kaplan explains the hit-or-miss aspects of her job on the Social Media Today website. "Content marketing connects your brand to your customer," she says. "Your work is either going to touch people's hearts and minds and connect with them in an emotional way or it will miss the mark."

While posting content on a regular basis is important, social media managers are also aware of when to post. For example, data compiled by social media companies shows that Facebook posts attract the most clicks on Saturday and Sunday afternoon, while tweeting is most effective around 5 p.m. on weekdays. Instagram is busiest on Monday and Thursday nights, and one of the best times to post videos to Instagram is 2 a.m. Social media managers also need to consider time zones when posting—2 a.m. in Los Angeles is 5 a.m. in New York. This around-the-clock schedule is why Rendler-Kaplan jokes that social media manager is a great job "for insomniacs." It is not necessary to stay up all night to do the job properly, however. Social media management tools like Hootsuite and Buffer allow users to schedule posts to Twitter, Facebook, Instagram, and Pinterest at preset times according to when the accounts are most active.

Posting content at an opportune time is not the only thing social media managers focus on. They are responsible for finding out whether the content they create is reaching its intended audience. This requires social media managers to keep track of analytics, which is information from websites and mobile apps about many things, including page and post likes, user engagement rates (likes, shares, comments), and user demographics (their ages, gender, and other personal data). This information is extremely useful when creating marketing campaigns for specific audiences, such as sports fans, moms, or college students.

Social media managers use numerous analytics tools, including Google Analytics, Snaplytics (Snapchat), Iconosquare (Instagram), and amaSocial (Facebook, Twitter, YouTube, blogs). An unnamed blogger for Portent Digital Marketing Services explains that these tools help social media managers "see what makes a post succeed or fail and why. I compare these stats by week, month, and year and decide whether or not the company is benefiting from its time and money spent on social media. If they are not, it then becomes a question of what can we do to make this more successful?"

How Do You Become a Social Media Manager?

Education

If you are interested in becoming a social media manager, you are probably already familiar with popular social networking services. But to pursue a career in this field you need to go beyond the habits of a typical user. As social media manager Alice Fuller explains on the Capterra website: "If you truly desire to be a really good social media manager, learn the fundamentals of marketing and writing first. Learn as much as you can . . . then put what you learn into practice for yourself, then work with others for free or [a] low fee so you can get some real experience under your belt."

Most high schools offer courses in creative writing and basic business tools, but there is a lot you can teach yourself about the growing and dynamic field of social media management. You can do your own research about the latest social media news and trends and learn about the algorithms that sites use to target ads and highlight the most popular posts. With this information you can perform the work of a social media manager by developing your own personal brand online. Join groups on social media that focus on one of your hobbies, whether it be horror movies or horticulture. Learn to engage in digital conversations, attract followers, and create content that produces likes, loves, and shares. You can also closely follow brands and companies you like while taking notes on various aspects of their social media campaigns. Correspond with the social media managers handling the brands, and ask them lots of questions. All this self-education can be accomplished in your spare time. As content writer Andrew Conrad explains on Capterra: "Social media management is more like music than dentistry: it's OK to learn it on your own."

Conrad points out that social media managers come from many different backgrounds and that there is no degree program in social media management that college students can pursue. Nonetheless, most employers expect job candidates to have a bachelor's degree in communications, journalism, graphic design, marketing, or a related field. While pursuing such a degree, college students can concentrate on creating portfolios from their Facebook, Instagram, and Twitter accounts. This provides a "living résumé" that will prove to prospective employers or clients that they know how to generate online interest.

Certification
Numerous organizations offer certifications that social media managers can obtain. Certification assures both employers and clients that you have what it takes to generate a successful social media campaign. Hootsuite Academy offers a wide range of industry-recognized certifications, such as Social Marketing Certification and Advanced Social Media Strategy Certification. Twitter Flight School certification can be obtained by taking a series of short, inexpensive courses that focus on statistics, case studies, and scenarios. Other social media certification courses include LinkedIn Marketing Certification and Facebook Blueprint Certification.

Volunteer Work and Internships
As Fuller notes, working as a volunteer social media manager is a great way to gain experience. And volunteering opportunities

are truly everywhere. Social media managers might begin their careers by building an online brand for a family or friend's business. Nonprofit organizations such as museums, theaters, and community arts organizations are always looking for volunteers to help them with online promotion. Jenn Scott, a digital marketing manager for a community college, told Capterra that students can probably volunteer at their own schools. "There may very well be opportunities to assist with campus social media efforts as a work-study or as part of a club or organization," she notes. In fact, Conrad started out by promoting his own business—a dog-walking service: "By turning that dog walking business into a successful Instagram account, I made sure that I had something valuable to put on my resume from that period."

Skills and Personality

Social media managers put the "social" in social media. They need to be genuinely friendly people who possess excellent communication skills. Social media managers spend their days engaging with consumers and responding quickly, but professionally, to their posts. The job also requires a creative eye and a meticulous nature to produce flawlessly executed, eye-catching posts. As Rendler-Kaplan explains: "[Social media managers] must aim to create interesting and engaging content, then take the time to chat with those people who spend their [time] engaging with you."

Social media managers also need strong math skills to understand complex analytics. They must also possess what is called emotional intelligence so they have a good sense of how their posts will be perceived by people from different backgrounds and viewpoints. In other words, social media managers must truly adhere to the adage, "Think before you post." An insensitive or offensive comment, even if unintentional, could end the career of a social media manager.

Employers

With the ever-increasing use of social media, there are ample reasons for companies to employ social media managers to expand their network presence. The main employers of social media managers include advertising firms, public relations agencies, political organizations, educational services, and nonprofits such as museums and theaters.

Working Conditions

Social media runs on a twenty-four-hour schedule, and social media managers often find themselves checking their company's social channels over breakfast or before they go to bed at night. They spend time scanning news sites for trending topics related to the companies or industries they are promoting. Much of the day is spent crafting engaging posts and analyzing marketing campaign performance. Social media managers also go to a lot of meetings. As Bugg says, "In my experience, social teams tend to be company nomads." In other words, they travel around the office, going from desk to desk to meet with public relations teams, marketing managers, e-commerce personnel, and brand managers.

Earnings

The US Bureau of Labor Statistics (BLS) groups social media managers with other public relations (PR) specialists. In 2017 the BLS reported that the annual mean income for all PR specialists was $59,300. That means that half these workers earned more than that, and half earned less. The lowest 10 percent of PR specialists earned less than $32,840, while the highest 10 percent earned more than $112,260.

Opportunities for Advancement

Social media managers can increase their salaries by moving into other areas of online marketing. Market research analysts, who study market conditions to determine potential sales of a product, can earn more than $63,000 annually. Those who become advertising, promotions, and marketing managers can make as much as $129,380 a year.

What Is the Future Outlook for Social Media Managers?

According to the BLS, job growth for all public relations specialists is predicted to grow by 9 percent through 2026. These job opportunities are likely to grow as more organizations discover the importance of enhancing their social media presence.

Find Out More

International Association of Business Communicators (IABC)
649 Mission St., 5th Fl.
San Francisco, CA 94105
www.iabc.com

The IABC provides career advice, certification, and webinars to business communications professionals. The association offers a student membership program that provides global resources, industry connections, and learning opportunities for those planning to work in public relations, marketing communications, and social media management.

Public Relations Student Society of America (PRSSA)
120 Wall St., 21st Fl.
New York, NY 10005
http://prssa.prsa.org

The PRSSA provides educational information and professional guidance to students who wish to launch a public relations career, which includes social media management. The society offers scholarships, publishes an online magazine, and promotes competitions.

Social Media Club

PO Box 1506
Millbrae, CA 94030
https://socialmediaclub.org

This club has over two hundred chapters throughout the world that promote social media literacy in the fields of education, journalism, publishing, and communications. The website features a book club, job listings, and a business directory.

Social Media Week

https://socialmediaweek.org

Social Media Week is an education and news site for media, marketing, and technology professionals. The website provides articles, blogs, and over two hundred hours of informational videos concerning social media management.

Computer Network Architect

The average person scrolling through a social media feed likely gives little thought to the massive computer networks behind Facebook, Instagram, Twitter, and other companies. These seemingly streamlined networks are actually the result of a massive complex of computers, servers, routers, network drivers, and software programs, which are overseen by people who work as computer network architects. These technical experts draw on their knowledge of telecommunications to plan, design, construct, and maintain data communication networks—the things social media companies depend on for their extensive cloud computing systems. Computer network architects spend their days conducting firmware updates, analyzing data traffic, monitoring for security

At a Glance

Computer Network Architect

Minimum Educational Requirements
Bachelor's degree in computer science, information systems, engineering, or related field

Personal Qualities
Analytical, detail oriented, good communication skills, business acumen

Certification
Cisco Certified Design Expert (CCDE) and Cisco Certified Architect (CCAr)

Working Conditions
Full-time work with some overtime required

Pay
$104,650 annual average salary in 2017

Number of Jobs
162,700 in 2016

Future Job Outlook
6 percent growth through 2026

breaches, and planning for future network growth. When expansions or changes are required, computer network architects use network modeling software to build test networks, which are then analyzed, tweaked, and perfected.

Computer network architects create local area networks (LANs) that connect computers in a limited area like a home or office. They oversee wide area networks (WANs), which link national or international networks. Computer network architects also build global area networks (GANs) that include satellite mobile communications technologies.

Computer network architects who work for social media companies often specialize in cloud computing. These massive systems, which make data available to billions of Internet users, are housed in data centers in multiple locations. On the Business News Daily website, tech journalist Ed Tittle explains the work of computer network architects who specialize in cloud systems in this way: "Cloud architects must understand the building blocks of IT [information technology]. These include client systems and applications, networking, infrastructure, data centers, programming languages, web tools and technologies, databases and big data. . . . In fact, cloud architects are usually experts in one or more of these technology areas or disciplines." These specialists might have job titles such as application architect, storage architect, database architect, or cloud architect.

Whatever their specific field of expertise, computer network architects at social media companies work with the most extensive computer systems in the world; for example, Facebook users view 8 billion videos a day, and the site provides around 600 billion page views per month. While Facebook does not disclose specific figures, experts estimate the company's cloud computing system depends on 180,000 servers. Meanwhile, Twitter operates hundreds of thousands of servers in data centers located on five continents.

The computer network architects that work for Twitter, Snapchat, and other social media services do more than design these systems. "Cloud architects . . . take ownership of such systems or environments throughout their lifecycles," explains Tittle. "Architects get involved with initial requirements analysis and see things through all the way to [equipment] retirement and replacement." This long-term commitment to a system requires computer network architects to look at the big picture and determine what their employers will need three to five years down the road. To predict a future system's features and needs, computer network architects create network models, analyze user statistics, and develop technology roadmaps that include system plans and expansion budgets.

Computer network architects also focus on security issues. Social media companies, which store personal information on billions of people, are under constant threat from hackers. Network architects establish security protocols, troubleshoot systems to ensure safety, and design backup systems in case of hacking breaches or natural disasters. This requires computer network architects to keep current on the latest IT security trends and procedures. As database administrator Kevin Hawkins puts it on the Cyber Security website: "You have to be on top of the latest and greatest technology or you're not going to survive."

In addition to their technical abilities, computer network architects need strong business skills. Their main job is to match the most cost-effective and efficient hardware and software with a company's long-term business goals. In this role, computer network architects interact with financial and marketing personnel and work with vendors to get the best deals on systems and software.

How Do You Become a Computer Network Architect?

Education
Employers of computer network architects expect job candidates to have a bachelor's degree in computer science, information systems, mathematics, physics, or engineering. High school stu-

dents considering a career in this field should take math courses, including calculus, trigonometry, and algebra. Courses that emphasize computer programming, physics, chemistry, and communications are also helpful.

College courses cover extremely technical subjects such as software-defined networking, network infrastructures, physical and virtual storage, data center computing, backup and recovery technologies, and disaster recovery. Some employers also require their computer network architects to have a master's of business administration (MBA) degree in information systems. Obtaining an MBA requires an additional two years of study in business and computer-related courses.

Like other IT professionals, computer network architects must constantly update their knowledge, as network analyst Justin Ryburn explains on the Network Computing website: "A network architect must have a thirst for knowledge and spend a fair amount of time reading blogs, listening to podcasts, attending trade shows and reading technical books to stay up on the latest trends."

Certification

Aspiring computer network architects can obtain different types of certification and climb up what is called the certification ladder as their careers advance. The basic certifications, Cisco Certified Design Associate (CCDA) and Cisco Certified Design Professional (CCDP), are aimed at those who work in networking and cloud infrastructure. Computer network architects can continue up the certification ladder by obtaining the Cisco Certified Design Expert (CCDE), which is a prerequisite for the Cisco Certified Architect (CCAr). At this level a computer network architect can also obtain the higher certifications of Cisco Certified Internetwork Expert (CCIE), Routing and Switching, or Data Center. Other senior computer network architect certifications include Salesforce Certified Technical Architect (CTA) and Red Hat Certified Architect (RHCA).

A computer network architect checks network servers. These professionals plan, design, construct, and maintain data communication networks that social media companies depend on for their extensive cloud computing systems.

Internships

College students studying to become computer network architects can find plenty of internship programs that focus on computer, network, or database administration. Internships are available at computer hardware manufacturers, software developers, telecommunications companies, educational institutions, and government agencies.

In 2018 computer engineering student Leonardo Babun was a summer intern at the Department of Homeland Security in Washington, DC, where he worked on security issues. On the Florida International University news website, Babun says internships give students the opportunity to learn what real professional life looks and feels like. "Quickly learn how to act professionally and be part of a professional team," he advises. He also urges prospective interns to take advantage of the opportunity to learn as much as they can. "Employers use internship opportunities to seek other very important values like a good attitude, honesty, hard work and team work. During an internship, be the first to arrive and the last one to leave, ask questions and try to integrate yourself into the team's life as soon as you can."

Skills and Personality

Computer network architects are often team leaders whose skills include the ability to communicate clearly and persuasively, in writing and in person. They run meetings, manage people of all skill levels, and must diplomatically explain highly technical issues to customers, managers, and executives, often while drawing diagrams on whiteboards. Computer network architects work with teams of software developers, security teams, and company financial officers. Tittle considers computer network architecture to be "both an art and a science. It's as much about understanding and accommodating the people who make use of computing and the services it can deliver as it is about the systems used to run them and the networks that tie them together."

Understanding the systems requires computer network architects to possess a strong scientific knowledge of computers, software, and digital systems. They have to be analytical and detail oriented to create comprehensive plans for networks. Organizational skills are also necessary to build precisely functioning networks from multiple parts. Computer network architects also need strong business acumen to understand their employer's business plans, budgets, and economic objectives.

On the Job

Employers

Many companies find it difficult to fill their computer network architect position because of the considerable education and work experience it requires. A LinkedIn study found that cloud architects were the second-most in-demand tech job in 2019. This means computer network architects can find numerous job postings by social media companies such as Twitter, Facebook, and Tumblr. Other types of employers seeking computer network architects include telecommunications carriers, insurance companies, computer systems design firms, educational institutions, and government agencies.

Working Conditions

Computer network architects work full time, and the job can be very demanding. According to the US Bureau of Labor Statistics (BLS), about one in four computer network architects worked more than forty hours per week in 2016. But those who work for large social media companies are provided with excellent benefits. Facebook, for example, offers free food, valet parking, on-call doctors, four months parental leave, and more. Similarly, benefits offered by Twitter make it one of the best places to work, according to the employment website Glassdoor. Twitter provides medical and dental benefits, generous vacation policies, catered breakfasts and lunches, gym memberships, laundry and dry cleaning services, and even on-site yoga and Pilates classes.

Earnings

According to the BLS, the median annual salary for computer network architects in 2017 was $104,650. Those in the lowest 10 percent earned around $58,160, while computer network architects receiving the highest pay earned more than $162,390. While the BLS gives median salaries from all industries, those at social media companies are higher than average. Computer network architects who worked for Facebook in 2018 earned between $116,000 and $144,000, according to Glassdoor. These employees also received financial benefits such as cash and stock options, bonuses, and profit-sharing plans.

Opportunities for Advancement

Most computer network architects work their way up through an organization. They often begin their careers as database administrators, computer systems analysts, or network administrators. After five to ten years working in the field with other IT people, skilled candidates may be promoted to the position of computer network architect.

Some computer network architects advance to the position of computer and information systems manager, a job commonly referred to as an IT manager. These professionals can earn more than $135,000 annually by planning, coordinating, and directing a company's digital activities. Computer network architects can also move up to executive positions. The job of chief technology officer (CTO) involves determining the overall technical direction of a company.

What Is the Future Outlook for Computer Network Architects?

The BLS predicts that the computer network architecture profession will grow by 6 percent through 2026, which will result in an additional 10,400 new jobs. The strongest growth will be in cloud computing, an area where many companies are focusing their IT investment.

Find Out More

Association for Computing Machinery (ACM)
2 Penn Plaza, Suite 701
New York, NY 10121-0701
www.acm.org

The ACM consists of computer science educators, researchers, and professionals who promote dialogue, shared resources, and recognition of technical excellence. The association promotes curriculum recommendations in IT systems, computer science, and software engineering from middle- and high-school level to undergraduate, graduate, and doctoral-level education.

Association of Information Technology Professionals (AITP)

3500 Lacey Rd., Suite 100
Downers Grove, IL 60515
www.aitp.org

The AITP, also known as CompTAI, is a professional organization with 62 local chapters and 286 student chapters at colleges and universities. The association offers webinars, conferences, and job listings to members, and its Student Program connects students to mentors and provides résumé support and career strategies.

National Center for Women & Information Technology (NCWIT)

University of Colorado
Campus Box 417 UCB
Boulder, CO 80309
www.ncwit.org

NCWIT is dedicated to expanding IT opportunities for girls and women. The center's AspireIT K–12 outreach program (sponsored by Google, Intel, and others) connects high school and college women with K–12 girls interested in computer science.

Network Professional Association

3517 Camino Del Rio South, Suite 215
San Diego, CA 92108
www.npa.org

The NPA is a leading organization for computer network architects and other network professionals. The association offers career advice, certification, and various publications useful to prospective computer network architects.

Influencer Marketing Director

What Does an Influencer Marketing Director Do?

Look at your Instagram feed for more than ten seconds and you will likely see a major celebrity, "microcelebrity," or vlogger promoting a product. They might be fashion bloggers, gym instructors, musicians, chefs, or even woodworkers, but they all have something in common: they are considered social media influencers. Advertising agencies pay them to hype products on Instagram, YouTube, and other social media sites.

The reason influencers are rife on social media can be traced to basic economics. According to the influencer marketing website Mediakix, a whopping 60 percent of YouTube viewers have made a purchase because of an influencer's promotion.

Because influencer recommendations can so dramatically affect a company's sales, 72 percent of major brands—including Macy's, Nissan, Uber,

At a Glance

Influencer Marketing Director

Minimum Educational Requirements
Bachelor's degree in marketing, communications, or business

Personal Qualities
Creative, social skills, analytical, organized, good communicator

Certification
Google, YouTube, or Hootsuite

Working Conditions
Full time in offices with regular overtime spent tracking trends on social media

Pay
$106,130 median annual salary in 2017*

Number of Jobs
249,600 in 2016*

Future Job Outlook
10 percent growth through 2026*

* includes all advertising, promotions, and marketing managers

Revlon, and Old Navy—said they were planning to significantly increase their influencer marketing budgets in 2019. This created a growing demand for influencer marketing directors. These professionals are sometimes called influencer relations specialists. They work for ad agencies and product manufacturers, and their job is to hire Instagram stars, bloggers, and YouTube celebrities (YouTubers) who can create social media buzz around their clients' products. Influencer marketing directors are skilled at finding influencers (sometimes called "talent") who have built their own brand online and who have a large audience of social media followers.

People who love to spend their time online might envy influencer marketing directors like Courtney D'Aiuto, who works for the advertising agency Ignite Social Media. As D'Aiuto writes on her company's website: "I don't play on Facebook all day, but I do get to browse through the various social media channels and unique blog websites on a daily basis. I'm usually looking for people who create and share relevant content online that could potentially fit well with the key messaging of a particular campaign I may be working on."

D'Aiuto understands the demographics (known in the trade as demos) of social media marketing. She works to match influencer endorsements with the most appropriate audience. For example, an influencer marketing director for a lipstick company might determine the target demo to be teenage girls between the ages of thirteen and eighteen. This would lead the marketing director to hire a beauty influencer like Michelle Phan, who hosts a popular YouTube video channel featuring cosmetics tips. A beer company might wish to target male sports fans between the ages of twenty-one and thirty-five, prompting the influencer marketing director to reach out to a popular blogger who writes about craft brewing.

Interestingly, young people are not always the most profitable demo, according to Joe Gagliese, influencer marketing director and cofounder of the influencer ad agency Viral Nation. As Gagliese explains on the Vox website: "A middle-aged audience is . . . a valuable demographic. . . . We work with this one influencer, Gerry Brooks, for example, who is a school principal and a Facebook personality with almost 1 million likes; 90 per-

An influencer marketing director talks to potential talent. These professionals hire Instagram stars, bloggers, and YouTubers who can create social media buzz around their clients' products.

cent of his followers are women who work as teachers, and are 35 and up. That is a unique, and lucrative, audience."

As Gagliese demonstrates, influencer marketing directors need to be experts when it comes to numbers and statistics. They track the success of each ad campaign and monitor all the platforms where their products appear. The marketers pore over data that includes views, likes, watch times, comments, shares, and engagement rates (the number of people that interact with the content). Influencer marketing directors also have to beware of hazards that can harm their clients. For example, some influencers purchase followers—that is, they inflate their engagement rates by paying services that use bots (apps that run automated tasks) to generate fake followers. This is unethical behavior, however, and influencer marketing directors caught using inflated numbers or otherwise purchasing followers might find themselves unemployed.

Numbers and statistics also play an important role in other tasks required of influencer marketing directors. They need to plan advertising budgets; negotiate contracts with talent, clients, and media outlets; and conduct market research studies to understand customer behavior.

Education

There are few formal educational requirements for the position of influencer marketing director because it is a fairly new job designation. But those who want to get ahead in this competitive industry should earn a bachelor's degree in marketing, communications, or business. High school students aiming to become influencer marketing directors can take elective courses like marketing, writing, and economics. Students should also build an extensive portfolio from their personal blogs, videos, tweets, photographs, and other posts while closely observing influencers that populate social media sites. On the Power Digital Marketing website, Sam Wormser explains how her early interest in influencer marketing helped her pursue it as a career: "Since influencer marketing and social media is something I genuinely enjoy in my personal life, it gave me a big leg-up when getting [a job] since I wasn't starting from scratch. I already knew how to use social media like a pro, I already followed a few hundred social media influencers, and I already engaged with them on a daily basis."

College courses in marketing focus on business law, management, finance, consumer psychology, computer science, math, and statistics. Courses that focus on digital or new media marketing are also important. Those who wish to start their own advertising agencies or work as consultants might want to pursue a master of business administration (MBA) degree in marketing. MBA courses concentrate on consumer behavior, brand management, product management, promotion management, and strategic marketing.

Certification

Employers of influencer marketing directors search for the most highly qualified candidates. Job candidates who are certified have a better chance of being hired. Those who are already employed can move forward with their careers if they upgrade their skills by getting certified.

Hootsuite, one of the most popular social media management platforms, offers several industry-recognized certifications. Candidates working toward the Hootsuite Social Marketing Certification can take a free social media training course online before they take the sixty-question exam to earn certification.

Understanding analytics is an important part of the influencer marketing director's job, and those who earn the Google Analytics Individual Qualification (IQ) show they are proficient in Google Analytics. Candidates can take online courses, including Google Analytics for Beginners and Advanced Google Analytics, in preparation for a seventy-question exam that requires a passing score of 80 percent.

Google owns YouTube, which offers the YouTube Certified program, created to educate all of that site's creators and users on how to succeed on the platform. YouTube offers three certifications covering areas like channel growth, content ownership, and asset monetization. Exams for each certification are about two hours long, and candidates need to correctly answer seventy-five out of a hundred questions to pass.

Internships

Marketing internships teach students how to take initiative, be part of a team, and learn the inner workings of the industry. In 2018 Eddie Brennan landed an intern job at Digital Brand Architects in Los Angeles. He sat in on meetings, discussed client brand strategy, pitched digital campaign ideas to clients, and calculated analytics. Brennan describes the positive aspects of his internship on the Hamilton University website: "This experience has taught me about compassion and the importance of learning how to work with so many diverse types of people. Whether they are mommy bloggers, fashion critics, body-positive models or personal trainers, every influencer has the opportunity to impact someone's life and help them feel a little more included, a little more confident, and a little more whole."

Skills and Personality

Influencer marketing directors are in the business of building and maintaining strong relationships. They communicate with numerous people every day, including clients and staff members. Influencer marketing directors often think outside the box, using creative skills to promote products in unique or unusual ways that will grab the public's attention. This requires analytical thinking to understand the latest trends and determine the most promising strategies.

Influencer marketing directors also use the art of persuasion to convince influencers to endorse products. They maintain relationships with those they have worked with in the past, while constantly reaching out to new influencers for future campaigns. This requires strategic thinking, as influencer marketing director Jordan Feise explains on the Traackr website: "Know what influencers your competitors are working with. Understand what influencers' motives are, what they stand for and the type of content they produce. Gain insight into what influencers work together or are friends in the space."

Successful influencer marketing directors spend a considerable amount of time following the latest trends, improving their skills, and updating their knowledge. As Wormser explains: "I know a few coworkers . . . who stand out as complete all-stars at our company, and I truly believe it's because these are the same people who are constantly talking about what they recently read, or a trend they did research on, or a new product or service they heard about and dug into. It's the people who have a thirst for learning that perform the best."

On the Job

Employers

Influencer marketing directors might be self-employed workers who develop a client base made up of local businesses such as restaurants, gyms, and boutiques. Others work for advertising agencies, while some start their own influencer agencies. D'Aiuto says she engages with personnel at major corporations: "[I have] worked with many household names; from food and beverage to personal hygiene, technology gadgets to greeting cards, charity events and more! You name a campaign and we've probably had a hand in bringing it to the masses via social media."

Working Conditions

Influencer marketing directors work with interesting, talented, and creative people. Shaping new campaign strategies and dealing with the latest social media trends is exciting and fun. As influencer marketing director Star, who works with fashion models, explains on the Fashion Fix Daily website: "Days can vary dramatically, but for me it tends to be building and maintaining all my Influencer relationships, which essentially is the basis of the job." Star feels lucky that she gets to spend her professional time on subjects and with people she genuinely likes. "I LOVE clothes, and the girls are such a huge, huge, huge inspiration. . . . I consider a lot of [them] . . . actual friends, although I may have only met them a handful of times." The job is not always as glamorous as some might think, however. Star says the work never really stops. She takes phone calls and responds to texts around the clock and watches vlogs before going to bed each night.

Earnings

The US Bureau of Labor Statistics (BLS) does not feature a specific job category for influencer marketing directors, but it does cover what it calls advertising, promotions, and marketing managers. People in these related professions earned a median salary of

$106,130 in 2017. The median salary is the salary at which half the workers in the occupation earned more than that amount, and half earned less. According to the BLS the lowest 10 percent earned less than $48,150, and the highest 10 percent earned more than $208,000.

Opportunities for Advancement

Influencer marketing directors who work for advertising agencies make great connections that might allow them to start their own agencies. Professionals in this position can also work more directly with talent as booking agents or business managers. Some might even go on to become influencers themselves, using their knowledge of sales, marketing, and sponsorship to promote themselves as Instagram or YouTube celebrities.

What Is the Future Outlook for Influencer Marketing Directors ?

The BLS predicts that employment for all advertising, promotions, and marketing managers will grow by 10 percent through 2026. Demand will be driven by businesses seeking to expand their market share on social media, which will require them to hire marketing directors who can introduce new products to the marketplace and plan, direct, and coordinate advertising and promotional campaigns.

Find Out More

American Association of Advertising Agencies (AAAA)
1065 Avenue of the Americas, 16th Fl.
New York, NY 10018
www.aaaa.org

This organization, known as the 4A's, promotes the interests of the advertising industry. The association's website features a large research database with marketing studies on nearly every industry. The 4A's also offers high school programs, certification, and online courses.

Influencer Marketing Association
https://influencermarketingassociation.org

This online trade organization was founded to promote influencer industry guidelines, provide resources to marketing professionals, and educate the public. The association features blogs, hosts meetups, and publishes a newsletter.

Traackr
244 California St., Suite 204
San Francisco, CA 94111
www.traackr.com

The website for this international influencer marketing agency contains a wealth of information of interest to prospective influencer marketing directors, including e-books, case studies, and infographics. Traacker also runs an education organization, Academy of Influencer Marketing, for marketers and agency personnel.

Word of Mouth Marketing Association (WOMMA)
10 Grand Central
155 E. Forty-Fourth St.
New York, NY 10017
www.ana.net/content/show/id/womma

This social media marketing association is part of the Association of National Advertisers (ANA) and provides over ten thousand pieces of focused marketing information, including articles on influencer marketing, case studies, and consumer research. The WOMMA website features over one hundred training webinars and offers several certification opportunities.

Artificial Intelligence Engineer

What Does an Artificial Intelligence Engineer Do?

The term *artificial intelligence* (AI) sounds like it was lifted from an old science-fiction story. While artificial intelligence is science, it is definitely not fiction. Artificial intelligence is defined as a computer system's ability to understand the real world without human input. Computers running AI programs perform tasks that would otherwise require human intelligence and labor.

Every one of Facebook's 2.3 billion users relies on AI when they see newsfeeds, search functions, and ads. Facebook also uses AI for services users never see, including facial and speech recognition, tagging, translating languages, and spotting fake accounts and objectionable content. In fact, Facebook's artificial intelligence systems handle

At a Glance

Artificial Intelligence Engineer

Minimum Educational Requirements
Master's degree in computer engineering, data science, or related field

Personal Qualities
Creative, business skills, perseverance, ability to grasp new concepts, and strong computer programming, data analysis, and math skills

Certification
Stanford Machine Learning

Working Conditions
Forty-hour workweeks with some overtime in offices with teams including electrical engineers, computer hardware engineers, and software developers

Pay
$114,520 median annual salary in 2017*

Number of Jobs
27,900 in 2016*

Future Job Outlook
19 percent growth through 2026*

* includes all computer and information research scientists

more than 200 trillion predictions every day, along with 5 billion translations.

Artificial intelligence, sometimes referred to as machine learning, is an integral part of all social media services, including Twitter, Instagram, and Snapchat. Social media marketers rely on AI to rate an influencer's power, analyze user engagement, and update content. Numerous other online businesses, including Netflix, Spotify, and Amazon, depend on AI to make playlists, create personalized recommendations, and perform other tasks.

It is safe to say that Facebook, Instagram, and the rest of the social media world would not exist without AI performing trillions of real-world calculations every day—and AI would not exist without artificial intelligence engineers. These professionals combine the skills of software engineers with those of data scientists to teach computers to perform complex tasks.

Artificial intelligence engineers perform data analysis. This means they detect and analyze patterns in very large datasets that might include billions of pieces of user data, including names, ages, phone numbers, addresses, bank balances, credit ratings, shopping histories, political affiliations, and more. A data scientist might present this information to other people, such as executives who manage a business. But an AI engineer will use the data to write algorithms (computer commands) that tell software how to perform autonomously—that is, without further human supervision. AI algorithms are also embedded in a variety of items, including computer chips, computer hardware, and cloud hardware, so that these machines can communicate with one another autonomously. Once the algorithms are in place, AI engineers test and monitor the accuracy of their models over time to determine when the programs need to be retrained or replaced.

AI engineers are among the most educated people in the workforce. They need to understand the fundamentals of computer science and programming to understand data structures (stacks, queues, graphs), algorithms (searching, sorting, optimization), and computer architecture (memory, cache, bandwidth).

AI engineers also have a strong grasp of probability—the likelihood that an event will occur—and statistics, which are used to build and validate models from data.

To perform their jobs, artificial intelligence engineers do a lot of reading. AI engineer Richard Waltman describes his typical work routine in a post published on the website Quora: "Read manuals for hardware (new and old), read language references to learn the inner workings of all available programming languages that are capable of [machine learning] . . . read dissertations and academic papers on [mathematical logic] and information theory . . . read and meditate on philosophy/math/physics/logic (often in German, Latin, Greek, etc.)."

Waltman calls himself an AI evangelist. In this role he advocates for the widespread acceptance and adoption of AI technology. He teaches people how machine learning works and tries to educate the public on the benefits of artificial intelligence. On a day-to-day basis, AI evangelists explain the technology to clients in terms they can understand. As AI evangelist Titash Neogi explains on the KDnuggets website: "I work with businesses to understand their needs or problems and suggest the right AI powered solutions for them."

The business role is an important one. Professionals in this field need to create artificial intelligence solutions that help their employers make a profit. They have to analyze market trends, observe what other companies are doing, and build systems that are better than those of their competitors. Attending meetings is another business aspect of an AI engineer's job. They work with colleagues to implement software and perform analyses, and they meet with executives to discuss updates and new products.

Artificial intelligence is a very broad field, and there are many different specialties within it. Those who specialize in data mining and analysis investigate large data sources and create and train systems to recognize data patterns. Some engineers focus on the application of machine learning to perform a specific function. This can involve training computers to recognize gestures, detect fraud, or analyze the content of ad and marketing campaigns.

Those who work as AI researchers study ways to improve algorithms and apply them to new domains. Yann LeCun, director of AI research at Facebook, finds AI research interesting because it is always yielding something new. "In the initial phase, a lot of research is exploratory: you have an idea, and you try it," he explains in a post published by the website Quora. "When things start to work, you can form small groups of scientists and engineers to focus on making the idea work and on applying it to real problems. If things go well, it becomes an engineering project."

How Do You Become an Artificial Intelligence Engineer?

Education

Social media companies that hire artificial intelligence engineers usually require job candidates to have a master's degree in computer engineering, data science, or related field. High school students who hope to become artificial intelligence engineers need to master complex subjects, including algebra, calculus, probability theory, statistics, and algorithms. Students who excel in these subjects can learn independently by searching for machine learning tutorials and courses online; for example, some online universities offer machine learning "boot camp": self-paced courses that can be completed in two to four months, with one-on-one weekly mentor support. There are also numerous podcasts like *DataHack Radio* and *Learning Machines 101* that provide insight into the profession.

College students who focus on artificial intelligence and machine learning need to take courses in computer science, artificial intelligence, robotics, physics, cognitive science, and engineering. They study database theory, database design, and operating systems like Windows and Linux. Students learn the database language Structured Query Language (SQL) and work with database management software like Microsoft SQL Server. Classes include storage technologies, networking, and database maintenance, recovery, and security.

Certification

Obtaining certification can help jump-start a career in artificial intelligence, improve a candidate's job prospects, and lead to higher salaries. The Machine Learning Certification offered by Stanford University on the Coursera website is among the top-rated sources of accreditation, according to a Quora survey of artificial intelligence engineers. This fifty-five-hour class, completed by nearly 1.7 million students and professionals, provides an introduction to machine learning, data mining, and statistical pattern recognition.

Other highly rated artificial intelligence and machine learning certifications are offered by Columbia University, Harvard University, IBM, Microsoft, and LinkedIn Learning. All of the courses are available online and designed to help beginners and intermediate students, as well as experts, excel at AI and machine learning.

Internships

Every social media company offers AI-related internships. These valuable opportunities provide potential talent with hands-on insight into the world of artificial intelligence. One example is the twelve-week Twitter for Students program, which fully immerses interns in Twitter culture. Each intern works with a mentor and helps bring new projects to fruition. Twitter hosts feedback sessions, developmental events, and social gatherings for interns.

Students pursuing undergraduate degrees who are willing to work in New York City or Los Angeles can enroll in the Tumblr intern program. Tumblr interns work in engineering, design, and marketing programs and have access to great perks while they do it, such as a relocation allowance and office-wide catered meals, and they have the chance to participate in valuable networking events with other tech companies. An engineering intern named Brendan expressed his satisfaction with the program on the Tumblr intern website: "Working at Tumblr has been educating, interesting, and above all, phenomenally fun."

Skills and Personality

Artificial intelligence engineers need to be highly accomplished at programming and data science, which requires strong math and statistics skills. As Fred Sadaghiani, chief technology officer (CTO) of Sift Science, explains on the *Forbes* website: "We are looking primarily for people who have a principled understanding of the statistics, probabilities, and math necessary to grasp the problem. That's the foundation of this all." Because the field is so new, artificial intelligence engineers must also be driven by curiosity and creativity as they invent novel solutions to new and emerging problems. The job also requires perseverance, the ability to spend months building models, testing them for flaws, and creating new and better iterations of previous failures.

On the Job

Employers

All social media companies, along with hundreds of other corporations, were eager to hire artificial intelligence engineers in 2019. This is in part because, as LeCun notes, large companies like Facebook have the monetary resources to fund long-term AI research. Outside of social media, major tech companies like Apple, IBM, Qualcomm, and Autodesk are looking for AI engineers. Transportation companies like Uber and the Toyota Research Institute were also hiring AI engineers in 2019.

Working Conditions

Artificial intelligence engineers work in teams with electrical engineers, computer hardware engineers, software developers, and other IT professionals. Most work forty-hour weeks, but the US Bureau of Labor Statistics (BLS) says that around three in ten regularly worked overtime in 2016 when facing deadlines.

Earnings

The BLS classifies artificial intelligence engineers as computer and information research scientists. The BLS says the annual median salary for professionals in this broad category was $114,520 in 2017; however, jobs for experienced AI engineers at Facebook in 2019, according to the employment website Paysa, were paying $257,846, while Twitter was offering $230,690.

Opportunities for Advancement

The job of artificial intelligence engineer is an advanced position attained by employees who might have started out as software engineers, data analysts, or other computer scientists. Some who work in the field move into pure deep learning research, get promoted to CTO, or start their own companies.

What Is the Future Outlook for Artificial Intelligence Engineers?

According to the BLS, the demand for all computer and information research scientists is expected to grow rapidly—19 percent through 2026. But the outlook for AI engineers might be even better than the BLS predicts since it is one of the most in-demand tech jobs. A 2017 study by the McKinsey Global Institute estimated that between 400 million and 800 million of today's jobs will be automated by 2030. As tech journalist Jan Krikke writes on Quora, AI is revolutionizing the business world: "In another 50 years or so, AI will have eliminated all jobs that require keyboards today. Most office work will have been taken over by AI. By the end of the century, people will look at pictures of today's call centers the way we look today at pictures of people digging the Panama canal [in 1904]."

DAMA International

364 E. Main St.
Middletown, DE 19709
https://dama.org

DAMA International is an organization that provides an environment for data professionals, including AI engineers, to collaborate and communicate. Its website section called "The Learning Channel" features webinars, certification programs, and other educational material.

DataRobot

www.datarobot.com

This international organization offers AI platforms for data scientists of all skills to build and deploy. The company's DataRobot University provides learning materials that include blogs, webinars, case studies, and white papers.

Institute of Electrical and Electronics Engineers (IEEE)

3 Park Avenue, 17th Fl.
New York, NY 10016-5997
www.ieee.org

IEEE offers students a wide range of learning, career, and employment opportunities. The organization's Standards University offers courses, games, videos, an e-magazine, and an e-learning library. In addition, the IEEE provides certifications for computer scientists and data professionals, including AI engineers.

KDnuggets

www.kdnuggets.com

This award-winning website focuses on artificial intelligence, analytics, data science, and machine learning. Prospective AI engineers can get a feel for the profession by viewing the site's webinars, tutorials, certifications, and job openings.

Software Engineer

What Does a Software Engineer Do?

It is no surprise that thousands of people want to work at Twitter, Facebook, and other social media companies. These organizations pay top dollar for talent and provide a wealth of perks from free dry cleaning to cash performance bonuses. But what type of employee are these companies looking for? According to a 2017 study by the employment website Paysa, software engineer is the most in-demand job title at Facebook, Twitter, and Snap Inc. (owner of Snapchat). This was also true at other tech and web-based companies, including Apple, Airbnb, Uber, Amazon, Google, and Oracle.

Software engineers create the programs that run computer applications and computer utilities and operating systems. These professionals are involved in the entire production cycle of a software program. Software engineers invent new ways to perform digital tasks. After an application is created, software engineers analyze and test the program to ensure it works perfectly. Performance

At a Glance

Software Engineer

Minimum Educational Requirements
Bachelor's degree in computer science, software engineering, or a related field

Personal Qualities
Strong math and programming skills, good concentration, analytical, strong communication skills

Certification
Microsoft and other vendors

Working Conditions
Laid-back atmosphere, experimentation is encouraged, flexible hours

Pay
Between $101,000 and $160,000 in 2017

Number of Jobs
More than 1.2 million in 2017

Future Job Outlook
24 percent growth through 2026

and security functions are added. After creating apps, software engineers create models, instructions, and diagrams called flowcharts that others can use as reference material for future upgrades.

Newly created software can have bugs or be difficult to use, which requires software engineers to go back through the design process and fix such problems. Once software is released to the public, engineers follow up on how it performs. They then further refine the program after reading users' experiences, reviews, comments, and complaints.

Software engineers often specialize in a particular area. Network software engineers focus on network architecture, network programming and analysis, and security. Lead software engineers have years of experience that enables them to work on complicated systems. They supervise other engineers and programmers, write code, coordinate work flow, and make final decisions on products. Software project managers are team leaders who oversee large-scale projects. They manage multiple development teams, hire and fire programmers, and write productivity reports for upper-level managers.

Those who specialize in gaming systems design actual video games as well as the software that runs the platform. Facebook, which owns the virtual reality (VR) company Oculus, depends on software engineers who combine the several specialties needed to create multiplayer video games. Oculus hosts an immersive, real-time gaming network, and multiplayer software engineers build applications that support thousands of users, all of whom are interacting simultaneously in 3-D virtual reality. Multiplayer software engineers design, implement, and maintain systems, build prototypes of VR interactions and architectures, and integrate network technology into applications. According to the Facebook job description on LinkedIn, multiplayer software engineers "relentlessly improve our online experience [and] suggest the best techniques to offer players the best network experience." These software engineers need extensive experience with 3-D simulation engines, as well as knowledge of security measures.

How Do You Become a Software Engineer?

Education

The terms *software engineer* and *software developer* are often used interchangeably, but there is a difference in the education required for each position. Software developers do not necessarily need a degree—there are some software developers who are self-taught programmers. Software engineers, on the other hand, need at least a bachelor's degree in computer science, software engineering, or a related field.

Prospective software engineers in high school can prepare by taking as many math courses as possible, including calculus, trigonometry, and algebra. Computer science courses that emphasize programming languages are helpful, as are classes in physics, chemistry, and communications. High school students can also sharpen their coding skills by visiting social media programming websites like CodeKata and TopCoder. These websites attract highly skilled coders who compete to solve puzzles and problems while sharing notes and methods after problems are solved. With nearly a million members, the TopCoder community provides expertise in many different areas.

Students pursuing an undergraduate software engineering degree complete courses in computer programming, program design, computer systems analysis, computer hardware, networking, information and database systems, mathematics for computing, operating systems, and data structures and algorithms. Software engineers who wish to work in research, start their own companies, or just earn a higher salary might also pursue a master's in software engineering. Two-year master's programs cover topics such as database design concepts, software system design, applied human-computer interaction, and software construction where students learn to build large-scale software systems like those used by social media companies.

Certification and Licensing

Software engineers who obtain certification stand out among their peers and gain credentials that help them land big promotions. While there are numerous accreditation programs, Microsoft certification is the most respected in the IT industry. Microsoft offers accreditation at two levels. The entry-level Microsoft Technology Associate (MTA) is open to high school and college students and provides certification in Windows development, software development, mobile apps, and gaming. Candidates must pass a multiple-choice exam before being certified. Students can prep for the test by taking courses in Microsoft training locations, taking certified courses in high school or college, or through self-study on the company website. The intermediate Microsoft Certified Solutions Developer (MCSD) certification focuses on web applications and application life cycle management. Applicants are required to pass four multiple-choice exams.

Those searching for independent certification can visit the International Association of Software Architects (IASA) website. IASA is the only program run by practicing software architects. Those who take online courses and pass exams can gain accreditation on four levels—Foundation (CITA-F), Association (CITA-A), Specialist (CITA-S), and Professional (CITA-P). Each level has a unique digital badge that can be shared online with employers and peers as proof of certification.

Internships

Most companies offer summer intern positions to computer science students who are studying software engineering. Candidates work with teams in a fast-moving environment to integrate, deploy, and support complex software systems. Interns participate in research and development, problem solving, maintenance, and other tasks. To qualify for internships, candidates must be enrolled in a college or university and be familiar with various operating systems, installation procedures, coding, and process management.

Internships at social media companies tend to be laid back and fun. Computer science major Yasmeen Roumie described her 2018 internship at Snapchat on the Chapter1.io website: "They don't restrict your creativity, so really anything you can think of is possible. We had some internal hackathons where whole teams would spend a day or two building whatever product they wanted related to Snap. I ended up getting second place at the intern hackathon for a product that encouraged users to engage with local businesses through location-based deals discovered in Snap Map."

Skills and Personality

Writing and analyzing computer code hour after hour—and relating to clients and other workers—requires technical talents, along with what are called soft skills, or people skills. On the technical side, software engineers need strong math and programming skills so that writing code becomes second nature. The ability to concentrate on extremely complex lines of code for long periods of time is also necessary along with an eye for detail; even the slightest error can result in an application performing poorly or crashing. An analytical mindset is useful for problem solving.

Good communication skills are a must, because software engineers work with developers, programmers, managers, and others. Good communication means expressing complex ideas clearly in plain English and listening closely to the comments, suggestions, and questions of others. Communication extends to writing, since software engineers are required to publish weekly progress reports and other documents.

Software developer Sergei Garcia says it is important to exchange information with others and remain open to new experiences. As Garcia explains on the website freeCodeCamp: "Whether it be by reading blogs, spending lots of time in programming related discussions, or even talking about what's new in web development during lunch breaks, being on the lookout for new things all the time allows the best developers to always stay ahead of the curve."

Employers

A 2019 study by LinkedIn found that there were more than eighty thousand job openings for software engineers. These professionals were in demand at nearly every major corporation, from Silicon Valley on the West Coast to Wall Street on the East Coast. They worked for social media companies, computer systems design firms, health care providers, and banking, finance, and insurance corporations.

Working Conditions

The work culture at social media companies is very laid back; experimentation is encouraged, and employees generally keep their own hours—those with children tend to arrive at work early while others show up at noon and work late into the night. And everyone can expect to work long hours when deadlines loom. Most begin their days going through emails from team members who need guidance or who have discovered problems with an application.

Software engineers need to remain focused on minute details for long periods of time. On a typical workday a software engineer will test, maintain, and monitor computer programs, review and scrutinize computer printouts to locate code problems, and develop new programs. Software engineers solve problems for less-experienced staff, attend management meetings, and work with programmers to expand or modify systems.

Earnings

The US Bureau of Labor Statistics (BLS) places software engineers and software developers in the same category. According to the BLS, the median annual salary for software engineers and developers was $101,790 in 2017. According to the jobs website Glassdoor, however, software engineers at Facebook were earning considerably more—$120,083 in 2019. In addition, software engineers at Facebook receive an additional $15,240 in benefits such as cash bonuses, stock bonuses, and profit sharing. Glassdoor said the typical Snap software engineer salary was even higher, $135,000 annually, with top engineers earning more than $160,000.

Opportunities for Advancement

Some who begin their careers as software engineers move on to become computer and information research scientists who create innovative technology solutions for business and other fields. Software engineers are also qualified to work as computer and information systems managers—also called IT project managers—who were earning more than $139,000 in 2017, according to the BLS.

Some software engineers advance into senior executive positions such as chief technology officer (CTO). Mike Schroepfer, who was CTO of Facebook in 2019, began his career as a software engineer. Twitter CTO Parag Agrawal followed a similar path, working as a software engineer before moving to the number two job at the company in 2018.

What Is the Future Outlook for Software Engineers?

The BLS says that there were over 1.2 million people working as software engineers in 2017 and that the employment outlook was strong. The BLS predicts a 24 percent job growth for software engineers through 2026. Employment analyst Benjamin Pring was excited by the strong job forecasts for software engineers, as he explains on CNBC: "If you're 16, or if you're 25, or if you're 35, trying to get yourself into one of those . . . areas is absolutely the right thing to do. There's clearly a huge demand."

Find Out More

Association of Software Professionals (ASP)

PO Box 1522
Martinsville, IN 46151
http://asp-software.org

This organization is made up of independent software developers who have created freeware and shareware. The website features the popular Portable Application Description (PAD) format used by over forty thousand software publishers to provide product descriptions and specifications to online sources in a standard way. Students can access ASP to learn from successful developers of desktop and laptop programs and cloud computing and mobile apps.

International Association of Software Architects (IASA)

12325 Hymeadow Dr., Suite 2-200
Austin, TX 78750
www.iasaglobal.org

The IASA is a community of IT architects focused on training, certification, and continuing education. Members can participate in instructor-led training or self-paced training to pursue an education in computer systems analysis and related IT professions.

Software Engineering Institute (SEI)

4500 Fifth Ave.
Pittsburgh, PA 15213-2612
www.sei.cmu.edu

The SEI works to help government and industry acquire, develop, operate, and sustain software systems that are innovative, affordable, and secure. The SEI website offers training and career advice and features an online library and certification programs.

Tech Dev Guide

https://techdevguide.withgoogle.com

This website hosted by Google is intended to provide tips and resources to university-level computer science students seeking internships. The site features Google's Guide to Technical Development with tools aimed at experienced programmers and advanced students.

Mobile Application Developer

Mobile apps are ubiquitous in the modern world. Apps allow users with cell phones and tablets to shop, listen to music, check their bank balance, follow the news, track their fitness level, play interactive games, and perform countless other activities. Mobile social networking apps from Instagram, YouTube, Twitter, Reddit, and WhatsApp are on billions of devices, allowing users to text, talk, shop, and post comments, images, and videos. Mobile apps have truly changed the world.

This explains why mobile apps represent big business. Each year over 180 billion apps are downloaded, and the mobile app industry was on track to generate $189 billion in 2020, according to the Statista website. That's more than two-and-a-half times what the industry generated in 2015. More people are now using mobile apps than desktop applications.

At a Glance

Mobile Application Developer

Minimum Educational Requirements
Bachelor's degree in software engineering, mobile application development, mobile computing, or computer science

Personal Qualities
Excellent coder, ability to concentrate, analytical, good business skills

Certification
Google Associate Android Developer, Salesforce Certified Platform App Builder, IBM Certified Mobile App Developer

Working Conditions
40-hour workweeks in an easygoing atmosphere with some overtime

Pay
$101,790 median annual salary in 2017*

Number of Jobs
831,300*

Future Job Outlook
31 percent growth through 2026*

* including all application software developers

Mobile app developers create software applications that run on phones and tablets. Before work begins, mobile app developers meet with development teams that might include market researchers, production managers, and business executives. User needs are analyzed, projections of public demand are made, and budgets are finalized. Once the need for a new product is established, the mobile app developer will create a list of desired functions and a rough sketch or graphic design of the user interface.

Most app developers build with the popular mobile design software called Appcelerator Titanium. This framework allows the developer to create what is called an application programming interface (API). This is a set of communication protocols and tools that renders the user interface and supports mobile functionality. Put in simpler terms, Appcelerator provides a strong working foundation for the basic functions of a mobile app. This allows the developer to concentrate on creating high-level features that might include account creation and app navigation functions, such as swiping left to see the next screen.

Mobile app developers are usually specialists who build apps to run on one of the major operating systems (OS) in use. Google Android makes up an astounding 88 percent of the mobile app market, according to Statista, while Apple iOS accounts for around 11 percent. Each OS has its own computer programming language and software development environment. Generally, Android runs on Java, whereas iOS requires developers to use a programming language called Swift.

When creating mobile apps, developers have to ensure that their programs are compatible with a wide range of hardware from older, smaller smartphones to the latest high-tech tablets. This requires them to build working prototypes that can be tested on different mobile screens. To do this, developers use several mobile app prototyping tools, including Sketch, Adobe Experience Design (Xd), InVision, and Framer. On the Appinventiv website, mobile app developer Srikant Srivastav explains the benefits of using app prototyping tools: "Mobile app prototyping, being the process that [shows] how your mobile application would look and function, is an amazing tool for sharing the concept with associates, the probable user base, and the investors. In addition . . . the prototype gives you the ability to gather feedback on how the app is [working]."

After prototypes are finished, app developers test them to ensure they don't crash, create bad user experiences, or cause security concerns. Mobile app developers sometimes use an independent testing service such as QualityLogic, which employs test engineers to ensure an app is bug-free and ready for release. If testers find an app difficult to use or flawed in some way, the app developer goes back into the design process to improve the program.

After an app is released, developers follow customer comments and reviews to further improve their product. Some might even answer user comments and provide solutions to individuals who are having problems with the app. App developers continue their work, creating patches for security and upgrades even while an app is being downloaded hundreds of time an hour.

How Do You Become a Mobile Application Developer?

Education

In a room full of mobile application developers, you might find people with associate's degrees, bachelor's degrees in computer science, and even self-taught coders. As tech journalist Melissa Thompson writes on the Axcess Business News website: "[The field attracts] people from various backgrounds including those with limited . . . experience. It's easier to transition from web development to mobile app development than starting from scratch. But with passion and dedication, nearly everyone can become an app developer." While people with limited experience can and do develop mobile apps, the job requires a talent for computer programming and a good understanding of the app market. And social media mobile app development is a highly competitive field. Employers seek job candidates with at least a bachelor's degree in software engineering, mobile application development, mobile computing, or computer science.

High school students can get a head start on this career by learning to code online. Codecademy is one of several websites that offers free basic programming skills. The digital education website Udacity features a number of free or inexpensive courses in mobile app development at beginner, intermediate, and advanced skill levels. Courses focus on basic Java programming, user interface design, data storage, and performance analysis.

College students pursuing an undergraduate science degree in mobile application development will take courses in computer programming, algorithms, data structures, logic and computation, calculus, linear algebra, and statistics. Other courses feature iPhone and Android app development, mobile video game design and programming, user interface design and usability testing, and mobile app deployment and marketing strategy.

Certification

Employers of app developers seek job candidates who have a strong grasp of various programming concepts and languages. Mobile app developers who get certified increase the odds that their résumés will be noticed or that they will be next in line for a promotion. Mobile development certifications are available from many large tech companies. The Associate Android Developer certification offered by Google is the most-requested accreditation by employers on job-listing sites like Indeed, LinkedIn, and TechCareers, according to a 2018 study by Business News Daily.

Those pursuing an Associate Android Developer credential focus on designing, building, and debugging Android apps. They take courses in design solutions for storage and designing applications to integrate with other apps. Certification is awarded after candidates pass a performance-based exam that requires them to create a project that showcases Java coding skills.

Mobile app developers can pursue other certifications, including Microsoft App Builder, Salesforce Certified Platform App Builder, IBM Certified Mobile App Developer, and Red Hat Certified JBoss

Developer. Apple does not offer official iOS developer certification, but those who are interested in that area can take short, immersive courses at Big Nerd Ranch boot camp.

Internships

Prospective mobile app developers can use an internship to enhance their coding, design, marketing, and business skills. And not all internships are unpaid; software development interns at Facebook were earning nearly $6,800 a month in 2018. Twitter, which developed a mobile app platform called Fabric in 2019, was offering software development interns about forty dollars an hour.

Around half of all internships lead to full-time employment, according to the Collegiate Employment Research Institute at Michigan State University. As Adam Ward, head of human resources at Pinterest, told the *New York Times*, internships are "a really smart way to recruit. It's all about trying before you buy."

Skills and Personality

With salaries that can top more than $100,000 annually, the position of mobile app developer was labeled "Best Job in America" in 2017 by CNNMoney, which said the career is low stress and offers personal satisfaction. Whatever CNNMoney might have to say about mobile app development, the work is not simple or devoid of stress. Coding software requires extreme concentration, and apps are expected to work perfectly, free of bugs, crashes, and security flaws.

Mobile app developers are creative, analytical, problem solvers. They rely on what is called spatial reasoning to visualize how various app functions relate to one another and how users will interact with them. Successful app developers are familiar with the strict manufacturer design guidelines that define how data is stored, how it is presented to the user, and how it is updated in response to user actions. Mobile app development also requires good business skills. Consumers expect apps to be free or extremely low-cost, so app developers need to understand how their products can make a profit.

Employers

Those who follow tech news might occasionally read a story about some ten-year-old who made a fortune by selling a home-made app on Google Play or Apple's App Store. In reality, few app developers make a living creating or selling their own mobile applications. Most work for Android and iOS app development companies, and social media companies are always looking for mobile app developers. In 2019 Facebook announced plans to integrate its social network's messaging services—WhatsApp, Instagram, and Facebook Messenger. This initiated a hiring binge at Facebook where hundreds of developers were needed to re-configure these popular apps at their most basic levels. Wherever a prospective mobile app developer applies for a job, managers will want to see his or her portfolio of mobile app samples.

Working Conditions

Most companies that hire mobile app developers have an easy-going atmosphere that allows employees to work at their own pace. And mobile app developers rarely work alone. Most spend their days participating in what is called a scrum—a management process for organizing and completing complex software projects. As Android developer Adam McNeilly, who works for HelloWorld, explains on his company's website: "[I participate in] a mobile scrum call with the entire mobile team. . . . During this call we go over what was completed in the last day, what we are working on today, along with a bit of planning to figure out what upcoming tasks are most important." McNeilly also participates in conference calls with other Android developers who work in different cities: "We call once a day to check in with each other about our projects and discuss the latest news in Android."

Earnings

The US Bureau of Labor Statistics (BLS) classifies mobile app developers as software developers. The BLS says the median annual salary for all software developers in 2017 was $101,790. The median salary is that amount that half the workers in an occupation earned more than and half earned less. The lowest 10 percent earned less than $59,870, and the highest 10 percent earned more than $160,100. According to a study by the employment website PayScale, mobile app developers who work for top social media companies can make up to $250,000 annually.

Opportunities for Advancement

Some mobile app developers begin their careers as freelancers and move into high-paying jobs at tech and social media companies. Others are promoted through company ranks to become systems analysts, video game developers, network administrators, or cybersecurity specialists.

What Is the Future Outlook for Mobile Application Developers?

The rapid growth of the mobile app industry has been compared to the Internet boom of the 1990s. And the expansion is expected to continue into the foreseeable future. The BLS predicts a 31 percent growth in all application software developer jobs through 2026.

Find Out More

Association of Software Professionals (ASP)

PO Box 1522
Martinsville, IN 46151
http://asp-software.org

This organization is made up of independent software developers who have created freeware and shareware. Students can access ASP to learn from successful developers of desktop and laptop programs, cloud computing, and mobile apps.

Codecademy

49 W. Twenty-Seventh St.
New York, NY 10001
www.codecademy.com

This online school offers free coding lessons in numerous programming languages, including Git, AngularJS, JavaScript, and CSS. Students can sign up and begin coding within minutes and learn the basics of mobile app development in a few weeks.

Software Development Forum

111 W. Saint John St.
San Jose, CA 95113
www.sdforum.org

The SD Forum is based in Silicon Valley and holds around twenty-five events monthly that are attended by engineers, mobile app developers, entrepreneurs, and tech experts. The forum provides information, education, and connections to those seeking to build a career in Silicon Valley.

TopCoder

www.topcoder.com

This website, with nearly a million highly skilled members, hosts bimonthly computer programming contests where mobile app developers, designers, and student programmers compete for cash prizes while solving valid problems.

YouTuber

What Does a YouTuber Do?

In 2017 British pollsters asked two thousand students between the ages of seven and seventeen what they wanted to be when they grew up. One-third of the students said they wanted to be full-time YouTubers—that's three times more than those who wanted to be a doctor or nurse.

Interestingly, the kids' parents were also surveyed, and a large majority had never even heard of the social media job desired by their children: "The rise in influencer marketing has been seismic, with . . . an increase in activity and sales across the board," says influencer marketing consultant Carina Toledo on the Telemedia website, "so it is not all that surprising that [YouTuber] is a genuine aspiration of many young people. . . . Whether we like it or not there is a place in the modern world for more unconventional jobs such as influencers and YouTubers."

The terms *influencer* and *YouTuber* are often used interchangeably, but there is a difference between them. An influencer might be a popular blogger or someone who promotes products to a large number of followers on Instagram, Snapchat, or Twitter. YouTubers,

At a Glance

YouTuber

Minimum Educational Requirements
None

Personal Qualities
Entertaining, good communicator, self-confidence, perseverance, video and computer skills

Working Conditions
Long hours to create, shoot, edit, and post videos

Pay
$12,140 to several million in 2019

Number of Jobs
Unknown

Future Job Outlook
Unknown

however, create videos that, among other things, try to influence viewers' purchasing decisions. So while most YouTubers are influencers, not all influencers are YouTubers.

Whatever you want to call them, YouTubers have attracted a lot of attention in the past few years from their work making vlogs (video blogs), gamecasts, tutorials, and other videos. When YouTubers provide links to product websites in their posts, they get a small amount of money for each viewer who clicks through to purchase the product. YouTubers also earn money from marketers for the marketers' ads that play before viewers can watch a video. Google, which owns YouTube, gets 45 percent of the revenue from each ad, while the YouTuber gets 55 percent. This can equal from around fifty cents to about five dollars for every thousand views a video attracts, depending on the YouTuber's popularity.

YouTubers make extra money selling T-shirts, hats, gift cards, and other merchandise. Some newbies depend on the kindness of their fans—earning money through the crowdfunding platform Patreon, a name created from the phrase *online patron*. As YouTuber Evan Edinger told the BBC: "Think of it as an online tip jar. . . . If you really like [the videos] and want to support them then you can pay something like a dollar per video, or a dollar per month." Sometimes YouTubers provide exclusive content to patrons.

YouTubers earn most of their money as influencers who are paid by corporations to talk about products and display them in their videos. According to a study by the social media ad agency Linqia, 39 percent of marketers planned to increase their influencer marketing budgets in 2019. Linqia found that marketers were willing to spend anywhere from $25,000 to $100,000 on influencer marketing.

Influencer marketing helped some YouTube superstars become millionaires. Jake Paul was worth $11.5 million in 2019; the comedy duo Smosh had a net worth of $11 million, and DanTDM brought in $16.5 million. The YouTube channel Ryan ToysReview earned $11 million—and it is run by a six-year-old named Ryan who provides reviews of toys to his 10 million followers.

While the money sounds amazing, students planning a career as a YouTuber need to do a reality check. The odds of becoming the next DanTDM are about the same as becoming the next Beyoncé or Lady Gaga. According to YouTube, one in every four channels is abandoned within three months because it takes at least six months to reach one hundred subscribers. Only one out of nine channels ever attracts five thousand subscribers. And YouTubers with such small numbers do not bring in advertising dollars.

While the odds of becoming the next Smosh are small, YouTube has a global audience of 1.6 billion users who watch an average of 4 billion videos every day. Those who can find a niche audience and attract millions of clicks can rise to the top, as social media manager Blake Stimac writes on Wix Blog: "The success of YouTube influencers of the past have made marketers shift how they can potentially reach their audience, so it's actually a very relevant dream to have for your own channel."

How Do You Become a YouTuber?

Education

Watching homemade videos on YouTube makes it instantly apparent that there are no educational requirements or any other barriers to entering this field. YouTubers do not need to get a college degree, present a résumé, pass an audition, impress a studio executive, or reside in a global media center like Los Angeles. That said, the most popular YouTubers are funny, engaging, and knowledgeable about their chosen subject. Their videos are high quality, on topic, and not rambling or boring.

If you dream of being a YouTuber, you can start by taking the following few steps. While some people have more natural on-camera talent than others, you can improve your chances of success by taking improv classes. These comedy workshops, which can be found in most major cities, help students develop quick reflexes and build self-confidence while fostering spontaneous creativity. There are also a number of summer camp programs, like the Start a YouTube Channel course, offered by ID Tech for kids aged thirteen through seventeen. Students learn to establish an online presence, make vlogs, capture and edit videos with professional equipment, and build a following.

If you want to become a successful YouTuber, you need to decide what sort of content you want to offer. Popular videos provide how-to instructions, humor, live gaming, political commentary, and reviews. Learn from others, check out what's already out there, and try to develop something that is uniquely yours. YouTuber Roberto Blake, who provides software education, offers this advice: "Write down 3 things you are good at. Write down 3 things you're really excited and passionate about. See if those things connect in any way and if they are similar. Pick one or two of those things that are VERY CLOSELY RELATED, such as Tech and Video Games. . . . Now think of what you would do if you had to [do] a TV SHOW around those ideas once a week. . . . Break down a beginning middle and end for your ideas."

Learn the economics of the influencer market and lay out a simple business plan. Visit YouTube's Partners Program (YPP) to learn the channel's guidelines and policies. Open a Google AdSense account, which tracks user clicks on each video and pays accordingly. Set up a YouTube channel. You might also need some video equipment. While some YouTubers start out using their smartphone cameras, viewers expect to watch high-quality videos. Consider purchasing a video camera, a tripod to hold it, a good microphone, and lights and light stands. A basic package can cost $500 and up. (The equipment used by popular YouTuber Casey Neistat cost $3,780.) You will also need an up-to-date computer to run the latest video-editing software. Details about the best equipment can be found (where else?) on YouTube.

Once you determine your investment and how much you can earn from your videos, you need to create a timeline for posting. Schedules are very important. Subscribers want to know when they can expect more content; for example, popular YouTuber Jenna Marbles posts a new video every Wednesday.

Then, create a list of topics you want to cover and write loose scripts for each video—even if you plan to improvise, you need to get to the point. Set up a "studio" in a corner of your bedroom, basement, or garage and think about decorating your set with interesting and attractive items.

Before you launch your channel, create five to ten videos that deliver value to your prospective audience. Whatever your topic, stick to it and make it fun. Remember that most viewers decide whether they will stick around within the first fifteen seconds. Remind your viewers to like, subscribe, and share your videos, and don't forget to promote your channel on other social media sites.

Skills and Personality

YouTubers are entertaining and informative, and are skilled at speaking in front of a camera. They have good technical skills and are able to shoot, edit, and post high-quality videos. Most post on a weekly schedule, which requires a lot of hard work and time management. And there is an element of anxiety, as game reviewer Matt Lees tells the British newspaper the *Guardian*: "It's not enough to simply create great things. The audience expect consistency. They expect frequency. Without these, it's incredibly easy to slip off the radar and lose favor with the [subscribers who] gave you your wings." YouTubers need to be willing to persevere, to keep creating and posting videos even when their subscriber numbers are low.

On the Job

Employers

Most YouTubers are self-employed entrepreneurs who create and upload content, promote themselves, handle all their user comments, and deal with the business aspects of running their channels. Those who achieve a measure of success hire managers or work with social media marketing experts to maximize their profits.

Working Conditions

Most YouTubers work nonstop to make videos for their demanding audiences. Many YouTubers feel they cannot take a vacation for even a few days. Those who take breaks might be dropped by the algorithms that decide which videos people see when they visit YouTube. As Fortnight videogame broadcaster Ninja told the *Guardian*: "I left for less than 48 hours and lost 40,000 subscribers. . . . I'll be back today . . . grinding again."

Earnings

The US Bureau of Labor Statistics (BLS) does not have a category for YouTubers or others who earn a living as influencers on social media. But the vast majority do not make big bucks. According to a 2018 analysis by Bloomberg News, 96.5 percent of all of those trying to become YouTubers earn less than $12,140 annually. This is considered a poverty wage by the United States government. Bloomberg also reported that those in the top 3 percent of most-viewed channels—with over 1.4 million monthly viewers—only earned about $16,800 annually. That means that 99.5 percent of YouTubers are not able to pay their bills from their efforts. As communications professor Alice Marwick told Bloomberg: "You can have half a million followers on YouTube and still be working at Starbucks."

Opportunities for Advancement

Some lucky YouTubers start off making videos in their bedrooms and eventually attract large audiences. Others go on to take more secure jobs working in social media management, influencer marketing, or related fields.

What Is the Future Outlook for YouTubers?

The BLS does not forecast growth rates for nontraditional jobs like YouTuber. In 2018 YouTube made some changes in the way that posters get paid that made life more difficult for small creators. The new rules state that creators needed to accrue four thousand hours of watch time over the course of twelve months and reach one thousand subscribers to earn money thorough its Partner Program. Since it takes about a hundred thousand views to attract one thousand subscribers, the future outlook for many YouTubers is uncertain.

Find Out More

ID Tech
www.idtech.com

ID Tech offers summer camp programs in numerous tech subjects, including digital video production. Prospective YouTubers can learn about various programs that might improve their social media presence.

Improve Effect
https://improveffect.com

YouTuber hopefuls can hone their talents through improv exercises. This website covers idea creation, skit presentation, and effective audience communication skills.

Los Angeles Film School
6363 Sunset Blvd.
Hollywood, CA 90028
www.lafilm.edu

Los Angeles Film School offers associate's and bachelor's degrees in majors relating to the entertainment industry. YouTubers interested in adding professional polish to their videos can learn camera, sound, and editing techniques.

Society of Camera Operators
2815 Winona Ave.
Burbank, CA 91504
https://soc.org

The SOC was formed to advance the art and creative contributions of camera operators and is committed to advancing the role of camera operators through educational outreach. YouTubers can gain insight about camera technology through this website.

Interview with a Social Media Manager

Tara Chambers began working as a social media manager in 2013. She has been director of marketing e-commerce at Scott's Marketplace since 2015. Chambers answered the following questions by email.

Q: Why did you decide to become a social media manager?
After college I traveled the world doing hospitality jobs. I transitioned into event management in 2008. I was living in New York, where I was fortunate enough to work with a team of web designers launching multimedia projects. After working with that team of awesome, innovative nerds, I knew that I wanted to learn and work in a field that was on the cutting edge and driven by technology.

Q: Did you study social media management in school?
I graduated college with a BA in english literature at Arizona State University [ASU]. When I decided to move into tech in 2008, I went back to ASU and entered into a program called Graphic Information Technology (which did not exist when I first went to college).

Q: How did this program help?
I was hired as an email marketing coordinator simply because I knew how to code. From there, I was drawn to the creativity of marketing and branding, and I also loved the data and analytics side. (There's nothing better than numbers showing that your efforts are working!) So I grew from my role as an email coder, to managing the department, and expanding our client contracts—ultimately being fully engrained with all channels of the marketing program.

Q: Can you describe your typical workday (or night)?

I'm happy to report every day is different! Reason being? Every campaign is different. Every season, every month, every day is different. Each and every customer is different, too. That means that you can't fall asleep at the wheel!

Each day, for me, has two consistent components regardless of where I'm working: collaborate with the team, and check your metrics! If bossman or bosswoman comes up to you when you're getting coffee in the morning, you need to already be knowledgeable of your current status (not yesterday's status when you left the office).

And collaborating with the team? I'm a firm believer that culture, interpersonal bonds and idea-flow are important, but also that time to do work is imperative. Therefore, the collaboration can take place in a variety of ways, whether it's a team meeting that's scheduled, or a quick shout-out on chat, or an impromptu coffee run. They all work, and they're all effective in their own way!

Q: What do you like most about your job?

I love it when we try out an idea and it works! It's an empowering feeling. I also love the flexibility that the marketing industry has provided for me personally. I love to travel. I like to work at night. Besides meetings, "marketing" isn't really a scheduled thing. As long as you're getting work done, and your work is done well and contributing to the objectives, I don't think anyone cares when or where it happens.

Q: What do you like least about your job?

Egos! Sometimes we all forget to check ourselves and no one idea is absolute. Try it, and let the data speak for itself! Be open to criticism. Be open to change. Learn from each other. Some teams can be a bit complacent in that arena.

Q: What personal qualities do you find most valuable for this type of work?

Bring some flavor, and show your personality. Say ideas out loud even if you think that they're "dumb." Chances are they will spark another idea either within yourself or the person next to you. You have to be fearless in that way, and know that every voice is equal and each idea shared is invaluable to the process.

A successful social media marketer also stays on top of trends in technology, marketing, finance, and pop culture. You never know when you'll have that opportunity to contribute your ideas and know-how in a setting that could change the trajectory of your career.

Q: What advice do you have for students who might be interested in a career as a social media manager?
If you are a combination of driven, creative, collaborative, and analytical, then this is the field for you. To succeed, use your voice. Don't be shy. There's no such thing as a bad idea.

Q: What are your current projects?
I just wrapped up a brand-launch contract where I set up their site, marketing integrations, and operational processes so that they can scale [up] when they have the budget to advertise and hire additional team members.

Other Jobs in Social Media

Analytics manager
Blogger
Brand ambassador
Chief technical officer
Communications planner
Community manager
Content manager
Content strategist
Digital communications
    professional
Digital media producer
Digital media supervisor
Director of public relations
    and social media
Information security analyst
Interactive media coordinator
Internet marketing manager
Manager of digital and social
    media
Multimedia communications
    specialist
Online communications
    director
Online content
    coordinator
Photographer
Social media account
    executive
Social media analyst
Social media designer
Social media editor
Social media evangelist
Social media marketer
Social media producer
Social media relations
    director
Social media strategist
Web developer

Editor's note: The US Department of Labor's Bureau of Labor Statistics provides information about hundreds of occupations. The agency's *Occupational Outlook Handbook* describes what these jobs entail, the work environment, education and skill requirements, pay, future outlook, and more. The *Occupational Outlook Handbook* may be accessed online at www.bls.gov/ooh.

Index